D1022056

I Don't Need to Have Children,

I Date Them

23 child psychology techniques
to use on boys of all ages

Karen Salmansohn
Illustrations by **Gary Baseman**
Design by **Valerie Wagner**

Workman Publishing, New York

Salmansohn, Karen
I Don't Need to Have Children, I Date Them.
23 child psychology techniques to use on boys of all ages
by Karen Salmansohn.
p. cm.
ISBN 0-7611-2217-6
1. Men—Humor. 2 Man-woman relationships—Humor.
3. Child-rearing—Humor.

PN6231.M45 S25 20001
818'.5407--dc21

00-069331

Workman books are available at special discounts when purchased
in bulk for premium and sales promotions as well as for fund-raising
or educational use. Special editions or book excerpts can also be
created to specification. For details, contact the Special Sales director
at the address below.

Workman Publishing Company, Inc.
708 Broadway
New York, NY 10003-9555
www.workman.com

Printed in Hong Kong
First printing May 2001
10 9 8 7 6 5 4 3 2 1

I'd like to dedicate this book to the warm, supportive, and just plain ol' always-totally-great-to-work-with-people over at Workman (or would that be WorkBOY?) who helped to give birth to this little baby of a book: Ruth Sullivan, Peter Workman, Kim Cox, and Elizabeth Gaynor.

—Karen Salmansohn

"The only difference between
men and boys
is the price of their toys."
—Anonymous

Contents

Introduction

Is Your Man in Touch with His "Outer" Child?

I'm not the first to say it. Time and again, psychologists have pointed out how many a man is looking for Mommy—well, except for those who are looking for Daddy. (But that's not my turf, so I won't even go there.) However, I will go—and have gone, and most likely will continue to go—into relationships that prove how in many ways men are just larger, hairier boys with more expensive toys. In fact, I've found the similarities between little boys and big boys to be quite startling. For instance, consider how child psychologists describe the development of a little boy's bonding style . . .

3-WAY
BOY BONDING

In the 1st year,
a baby will
communicate solely on
a physical level.

In the 2nd year,
he'll communicate verbally.

And in the 3rd year,
he'll use his verbal skills
to fight with you.

Chances are, you've already noticed how the above also holds true for big boys—except these stages are often acted out in months, not years. And that's just the beginning of the similarities between little boys and big boys.

BIG BOYS, LITTLE BOYS . . .

IS THERE A
DIFFERENCE?

Both share a major breast fixation.

They can actually be cute when bald.

(Unfathomably.)

Both
prefer the
naked state
of being . . .

and have trouble
dressing themselves.

Both hope to pass off the act of belching as something adorable.

Ditto with farting.

Little boys/
big boys **love**
cute teenage girl
baby-sitters.

(And in particular love
sitting on their laps.)

Both do things that inspire you to spank them.

They are into playing games . . .

LET'S PLAY HIDE + SEEK.
I'LL HIDE AND YOU SEEK ME.

CATCH ME IF YOU CAN.

. . . and **are** shameless flirts.

Big boys/ little boys get very cranky when they want to go to bed.

(And are known for keeping you up all night with their moaning and screaming.)

Both . . .

love to be told, You are

sooooo
big.

. . . think
the Three Stooges
are funny.

. . . have
been
known
to need
potty
training.

Both **have trouble** communicating . . . uh . . .

. . . emotions **in complete sentences.**

Little boys/
big boys
make
women
want to
cuddle
them.

(No matter how much
baby fat they're sporting.)

Both can make
women love them,
no matter
what they do.

OOPS

(Even if they break
something hard
to replace—
um, say, like
your heart.)

Boy oh boy! Man oh man! In other words, isn't it amazing how much little boys have in common with big boys? But this is not a reason to fret. In fact, quite the opposite. Now here's the Good News and the Even Gooder News.

THE GOOD NEWS:

BECAUSE BIG BOYS AND LITTLE BOYS HAVE SO MUCH IN COMMON, ONCE YOU MASTER A FEW CHILD PSYCHOLOGY TECHNIQUES, YOU CAN FIX ANY BOO-BOOS YOU HAVE IN YOUR RELATIONSHIP AND MAKE EVERYTHING ALL BETTER.

THE EVEN GOODER NEWS:

I'VE ALREADY DONE THE HARD WORK FOR YOU. THE NEXT SECTION IS FILLED WITH NIFTY TRICKS FROM CHILD-REARING EXPERTS THAT YOU CAN USE—AND THEREBY ENSURE THAT YOUR MAN ENJOYS A HAPPY SECOND CHILDHOOD.

CHILD
PSYCHOLOGY
TECHNIQUES

FOR BOYS OF
ALL AGES

Always make your boy feel in control.

When your boy refuses to do what you say, he is displaying independence issues. To help him feel in control, give him a choice of two things—knowing that he'll usually choose the second thing because he heard it last. Use this to your advantage. For instance, ask:

"Would you like to go for Chinese food tonight . . .

or . . .

Would you rather marry me?"

Always explain the WHY behind a CAN'T.

Get your boy involved in understanding the reasoning behind a no-no.
It will build his self-esteem and a healthy independence.
For instance, say:
"You can't touch
that radiator
and/or
that tall Swedish stewardess
because you will
get burned
and/or
get your pee-pee lopped off."

Terminate or distract:
the two best ways
to handle a cranky
boy.

If your boy is screaming—
either leave the room until he
calms down or distract him.
For instance . . .
try speaking very softly.
When he sees your lips move,
he will stop screaming
out of curiosity to hear you.
If that doesn't work,
try sticking a nipple in his mouth.

Food and rest can solve most problems.

If your boy has a bad case of the "crankies," chances are he's either overtired or hungry. If it's the latter, make him a favorite treat. I recommend the following recipe for Peanut Butter and Jelly Balls:

- one cup chunky peanut butter
- one cup grape jelly
- one cup Rice Krispies
- five tablespoons brown sugar

Mix the above in a large bowl until all ingredients are evenly distributed. Roll into half-inch balls and refrigerate for an hour. (Add crushed nuts and/or Valium for even faster results.)

Find out what's behind your boy's moodiness.

If neither food nor rest
fixes your boy's bad mood,
figure out what will.
Your boisterous boy may
be trying to tell you:

Yo. I need to feel important.
Hmph. I feel a lack of control.
Egads. I have too many choices.
Grrrr. I have too many limits.

Also, remember:

Bad moods are contagious.
Is he getting his from you?

Get to the root of his
problem— and deal with
the cause, not the symptom.

Never ask questions your boy can reject.

You can avoid the risk of an ego battle by asking questions that ensure your needs will be met. For instance, DON'T ask:
"Sweetie, can we stop watching baseball and go to the museum?"
DO ask:
"When we go to the museum today, do you want to visit the Egyptian wing or the Cartier exhibit?"

Speak in Happy Talk whenever possible.

Always adopt the positive position with your boy. When you purposefully choose positive, cheery words and expressions, you create a subliminal positive and happy environment.

For instance . . . never say: "Don't you %$# dare go into that stupid topless club ever again."

Instead, DO say: "Please go into nice restaurants where the waitresses wear all their pretty clothes."

Let him know truth-telling pays by never over-reacting.

Never grill your boy. Instead, set up a safe place for openness. For instance, if he says, "Sue bit me," you should respond warmly, not angrily, with a "Really? How'd that happen, honey?" Soon he'll be bursting to tell you important details, like "Well, first I tickled Sue, then she licked me, then I nibbled on her, then she bit me!"

TECHNIQUE EIGHT

Turn changing behavior into a fun game.

You can encourage your boy to change his behavior by turning what you want him to do into a playful game. For instance, if you feel he is not behaving "appropriately" at bedtime, try setting up a challenge, like "I betcha can't play with me— and this fun plastic vibrating toy— for thirty minutes without falling asleep!" You will then set up an incentive for him to want to play with you, so he can:

1. win
2. prove you wrong

—the 2 Top Boy Life Motivators

(next to Peanut Butter and Jelly Balls. See page 53 for recipe).

Use praise and reward to your advantage.

Boys learn early that being GOOD gets them LESS attention than being NAUGHTY. For instance, if you're busy, busy, busy, your boy knows the only way to get your attention is to mess up things (e.g., the house or your relationship). So catch him being good and praise or reward him with a big bubble bath!

Don't let your boy manipulate you with his cuteness.

Remember, the first few months that he spent with you, you spent googling over how utterly cute he is. He knows—subconsciously or consciously—that when he misbehaves all he has to do is pop out the boo-boo pouting lip and you'll cave. Don't. Be lovingly unbending. Often he is misbehaving to test you. This is not a test you can afford to fail, even once, or he won't think twice about breaking more rules.

Encourage your boy's interest in erections and discourage his penis worries. **(Duh.)**

Don't nag, scold, or beg your boy into giving you more hugs and kisses.

Don't take it personally if your boy is suddenly resistant to affection. He is simply going through a period of independence. Making him feel guilty won't win you more love. Be patient—and keep in mind that right before and after naptime, bedtime, and bathtime, your boy will be most open to physical affection. Take advantage of such times!

underactivity boy

super-high-activity boy

distractible boy

oversensitive boy

Know Your Boy

Don't expect your boy to change 100%. Try 20%.

You must accept that your boy has his own innate character and temperament flaws. At best, you can expect what psychologists call a 20% shift in "temperament heritage." So, be honest with yourself about who your boy is when making plans, buying gifts, or taking trips.

TECHNIQUE FOURTEEN

Know that setting limits shows your love (and gets you more goodies).

Psychologists all agree: a disciplined child is a happier child. This is because your boy recognizes— on a subconscious level— that when you take the time to discipline him, you are showing that you care. He will respond by showing his appreciation, in his own little ways.

You don't always have to win.

Discipline shouldn't be a series of wins and losses between you and your boy. Discipline should leave room for compromise. If he wants to play every time you're late for work, let him win some snuggles on occasion. Beware: too many "no's," and your boy will always be on the defensive.

TECHNIQUE SIXTEEN

For each NO you give, always offer a YES in the form of a playful alternative.

For instance, try saying, "No, you **CANNOT** stay out all night with your friends drinking cheap beer and painting the town red. **HOWEVER...** you **CAN** stay up all night drinking expensive wine with me and painting my toenails pink."

Explore the fun of reverse psychology!

If your boy isn't doing what you want, you can beat him at his own game by telling him to do what you DON'T want him to do.

NOTE: Be careful not to use reverse psychology in an area that could risk his safety.

For instance, DO NOT say: "Please have sex with as many drug-toting (and -tooting) prostitutes as you want! Yessiree, I just love it when you do that!"

TECHNIQUE EIGHTEEN

Don't let your boy watch too much tv.

Instead give him lots of t and p (talking and playing). Remember there is a difference between being in the same room with your boy and interacting with your boy. (And no, passing yummy cookies back and forth on the couch does NOT count as interaction!)

Prepare your boy positively for all shopping trips.

Don't start scolding him for Potential Shopping Misbehavior before you've even left the house. Instead, be positive about your shopping trip, as if it's going to be oodles of fun. Then try to make it so. When in the store, let him push the cart or play peek-a-boo in the dressing room.

To improve your boy's communication skills, improve your listening skills.

Even if you don't have the foggiest idea what he is trying to communicate, don't interrupt. Instead, respond with "Hmmm, that's interesting," just to keep him talking. Pay attention to facial expression and body language. Researchers have also found that asking questions is the best way to spur language development.

= The "I'm happy" face

 = The "I'm sad" face

 = The "Uh-oh, I gotta pee" face

TECHNIQUE TWENTY-ONE

Leave melodramatic departures and arrivals to the movies.

If your boy is displaying clinginess, don't subconsciously encourage dependent behavior by making a big good-bye scene at the door. Always use a calm and casual tone whenever you go out or arrive home. If possible, use the same exact words (e.g., "Bye-bye, sweetie pie" and "Hi, honey, I'm home"). If you establish Consistent Departure and Return Rituals, he'll soon feel more trusting and comfortable about your comings and goings.

Remember to follow the P.A.L. guidelines with your boy on a daily basis.

P — is for patient, even when you don't want to be.

A — is for approachable, so he feels it's safe to talk to you at all times.

L — is for lots of love, which you should always be showing and telling.

SOME
MATERNAL
WISDOM

TO GO...

Now you know everything there is to know about that

mysterious species called BOY. Well, almost everything.

There is one more thing you need to know. And even I

don't know what that is. You need to research this thing on

your own. In other words, it's up to you to find out

what your boy's original mom is like. By finding out every-

thing you can about your boy's first mommy, you can prepare

yourself for the following 2 Potential Mommy Problems:

2 POTENTIAL MOMMY PROBLEMS

1. You will remind him too much of his original mommy.
2. **You won't remind him enough of his original mommy.**

Either way, it is best to know what you are up against. Plus, you should keep in mind that whatever were the major problems his original mom endured will become the top problems you should be on the lookout for.

That's all. Now I must go bye-bye.